The Split History of the

BATTLES OF LEXINGTON AND CONCORD:

BRITISH PERSPECTIVE

BY BRENDA HAUGEN

CONTENT CONSULTANT:
Walter R. Borneman
Historian and Author of
American Spring: Lexington, Concord, and the Road to Revolution

COMPASS POINT BOOKS
a capstone imprint

About the Author

Award-winning journalist Brenda Haugen has written more than 50 books and edited hundreds more. She loves history, and the Boston area is one of her favorite places to visit. She enjoys traveling, hockey, and spending time with friends and family, which includes her two rescue dogs, Jake and Alice.

Source Notes

Patriot's Perspective:

Page 12, line 7: Samuel Adams. *The Writings of Samuel Adams: 1773–1777. Vol. 3.* Harry Alonzo Cushing, ed. New York: G. P. Putnam's Sons, 1907, p. 211.

Page 12, line 20: David Hackett Fischer. *Paul Revere's Ride.* New York: Oxford University Press, 1994, p. 95.

Page 18, line 4: Frank Warren Coburn. *The Battle of April 19, 1775.* Boston, Mass.: F.L. Coburn & Co. 1912, p. 31.

Page 19, line 16: *Paul Revere's Ride,* p. 191.

Page 19, line 22: *Journals of the Continental Congress, 1774–1789.* Worthington C. Ford, et al, eds. Washington, D.C.: Library of Congress, 1904–1937, p. 31.

Page 24, line 1: *Paul Revere's Ride,* p. 209.

Page 24, line 5: Ibid., p. 210.

Page 24, line 13: Ellen Chase. *The Beginnings of the American Revolution: Based on Contemporary Letters, Diaries, and Other Documents, Vol. III.* New York: Baker and Taylor Company, 1910, p. 39.

Page 28, line 16: Charles Knowles Bolton, ed. *Letters of Hugh, Earl Percy, from Boston and New York, 1774–1776.* Boston: Charles E. Goodspeed, 1902, p. 52–53.

British Perspective:

Page 9, line 8: "Letter from Governour Gage to the Earl of Dartmouth, August 27, 1774." American Archives: Documents of the American Revolutionary Period 1774–1776, p. V1:742. 11 Oct. 2017. http://amarch.lib.niu.edu/islandora/object/niu-amarch%3A93419

Page 11, line 8: Thomas P. Slaughter. *Independence: The Tangled Roots of the American Revolution.* New York: Hill and Wang, 2014, p. 411.

Page 14, line 3: John R. Galvin. *The Minute Men: The First Fight: Myths and Realities of the American Revolution.* Washington, D.C.: Potomac Books, Inc., 2006, p. 100.

Page 15, line 11: "A British Officer in Boston in 1775." *The Atlantic Monthly,* Volume 39, Issue 234. Boston: H.O. Houghton and Company, April 1877, p. 398.

Page 15, line 22: Ibid., p. 398.

Page 17, line 2: Ibid., p. 398.

Page 18, line 2: Ibid., p. 399.

Page 20, line 11: "Mary Prescott Barrett Interview with Shattuck 1831." Barrett Farm Historic Structure Report—Appendix. 17 Feb. 2008, p. 64. 11 Oct. 2017. https://www.nps.gov/mima/learn/historyculture/upload/Barrett-Farm-HSR-Appendix-Creduced.pdf

Page 21, line 3: Frederic Hudson. "The Concord Fight." *Harper's New Monthly Magazine.* December 1874–May 1875, p. 797.

Page 24, line 4: *The Atlantic Monthly,* April 1877, p. 400.

Page 26, line 23: *Letters of Hugh, Earl Percy, from Boston and New York, 1774–1776,* p. 54.

Page 27, line 4: Mackenzie, Frederick, and Allen French, ed. *A British Fusilier in Revolutionary Boston.* Cambridge, Mass.: Harvard University Press, 1926, p. 56.

Page 29, line 9: *Journals of the American Congress from 1774 to 1788, Vol. 1,* Washington, D.C.: Way and Gideon, 1823, p. 67.

Table of Contents

SHARED RESOURCES

CHAPTER 1
EXERTING CONTROL

*W*as it a top-secret mission or just another training exercise?

The British troops—and many of their officers—didn't know.

Whatever it was, it started around 10 p.m. on April 18, 1775.

Under the command of Lieutenant Colonel Francis Smith, the

soldiers had quietly met on a remote beach in Boston's Back Bay

section. The British navy had supplied boats to carry the men across

the Charles River to Lechmere Point in Cambridge. But there

weren't enough boats to carry all the men at once. The boats would

have to make two trips.

Hours later, when all the men had reached the shore in Cambridge, the soldiers struggled to get in formation. By then, they were already significantly behind schedule.

Finally, as they marched forward, they discovered another challenge—Lechmere Point was a very swampy area. Getting their footing proved difficult and even dangerous along the river's edge, and walking in swamp water up to their waists was even more unpleasant. By the time they reached firm ground, the troops were shivering in their wet uniforms as a chilly April wind blew through the New England town. Despite their misery, they had to wait there another hour until the navy delivered their supplies.

LESS THAN FANCY FOOTWEAR

Members of the British infantry wore unusual footwear in 1775. They didn't have left or right shoes. Instead, they wore heavy, square-toed shoes that could be worn on either foot. They switched the shoes from foot to foot each day so they wouldn't become crooked. The soldiers on the mission to Concord were expected to march 40 miles (64 kilometers) round-trip in these shoes.

Around 2 a.m., four hours after leaving Boston, Smith ordered his troops to resume their march. Smith knew their destination was the stores of weapons in Concord, Massachusetts, nearly 20 miles (32 km) away. The element of surprise was key to the success of the mission. But with the troops already hours behind schedule, the chances of them making it to Concord and back without being detected were dwindling.

A TENSE TIME

Tensions between British authorities and colonists—particularly in Massachusetts—had been growing for years. The French and Indian War (1754–1763) had been costly, and the British expected the American colonists to help pay off the debt. But the taxes levied against the colonists were met with anger, particularly in Boston, even when the taxes were small.

The French and Indian War was fought between the French and British and their Native American allies. American colonists also sided with the British.

THE FRENCH AND INDIAN WAR

The French and Indian War (1754–1763) was a conflict between Great Britain and France for control of North America. Many future American leaders, including George Washington, fought with the British during the French and Indian War and gained valuable battle experience. When the war ended in 1763 with a British victory, Great Britain took control of territories in Canada from the French and received Florida from Spain.

British authorities hoped a show of force in Boston would keep the situation from growing into a full-scale rebellion. In September 1768 a fleet of British ships sailed into Boston Harbor. The ships' cannons were pointed directly at Boston, so there was no mistaking the intent. The ships also carried two regiments of British soldiers meant to maintain order in the community.

But the arrival of the soldiers only increased the level of anger and unrest in Boston. Some rebellious colonists didn't respect the troops and sometimes assaulted them—often only with harsh words but at other times with physical actions. On March 5, 1770, the colonists' anger turned violent. That night an angry mob of colonists surrounded a group of British soldiers. Fearing for their lives, the soldiers fired into the crowd. Three people were killed instantly, and two others died later from their injuries in what came to be known as the Boston Massacre.

The Boston Massacre started with colonists throwing snowballs at a British guard.

After the Boston Massacre, Parliament tried to bring peace to Boston. The Townshend Acts were among the taxes that had angered the colonists. Passed in 1767, the Townshend Acts taxed paper, paint, glass, and lead. They also included a tax on tea that was so small that British officials believed the colonists wouldn't object to it. After the massacre, Parliament repealed the Townshend Acts—all but the small tax on tea.

But when three ships carrying tea for the British East India Company arrived in Boston Harbor in 1773, the American rebels were quick to show their continued anger. Dressed as Native Americans, the rebels boarded the ships and dumped 342 chests of tea into the harbor. The incident came to be known as the Boston Tea Party.

Parliament responded with the Coercive Acts. Under the acts, the port of Boston was closed and most town meetings were banned. Still hoping for a peaceful resolution, the British hoped the new laws would rein in the rebels.

CHAPTER 2

THREATS TO PEACE

he British saw the colonists' acts of rebellion as threats to

peace. British officials hoped the arrival of General Thomas Gage in

Boston in May 1774 would calm the situation. England's King

George III had made Gage the governor of Massachusetts. For the

first few weeks, Gage believed he would be able to subdue the rebels.

But after a few weeks, his hopes were dashed.

In August he sent a letter to the secretary of state for the colonies

expressing his concerns: "In Worcester [Massachusetts] they . . . have

General Thomas Gage took charge of the British troops in North America in 1763 and was named the military governor of Massachusetts in 1774.

been purchasing arms; preparing them; . . . providing powder;

and threaten to attack any troops who dare oppose them . . .

I [fear] that I shall soon be obliged to march a body of troops

into that township, and perhaps into others . . . to preserve

the peace."

By February 1775 Parliament declared the colony of Massachusetts to be in a state of rebellion. Gage was expected to take care of it.

TRYING TO AVOID CONFLICT

Gage was slow to act. In early April he was still hoping he could wait until reinforcements were sent from Great Britain. At the time, Gage had only 3,500 soldiers. With additional troops, he could consider making more aggressive moves to enforce the laws passed by Parliament. Without reinforcements, Gage did not believe he could stop a rebellion. He once remarked, "If force is to be used at length, it must be a considerable one, and foreign troops must be hired, for to begin with small numbers will encourage resistance . . . and will in the end cost more blood. . . ."

In the meantime, Gage had to listen to complaints from some of the few loyalists in the colony as well as from junior officers. They all thought his order to refrain from fighting colonists who taunted the British troops was ridiculous. But Gage was trying to avoid violence. He still held out hope that things would calm down in the colony. If not, he feared a small skirmish in Boston might lead to a bigger battle and spread to other colonies.

DEMANDING ACTION

Finally, British officials in London had had enough. They told Gage he needed to act. Reluctantly, Gage put together a military response. He had heard that rebels were gathering stores of weapons and other supplies in Concord, about 20 miles (32 km) northwest of Boston. Gage decided he would send his troops on a secret mission to destroy the weapons.

At 10 p.m. on April 18, 1775, Gage gathered his troops on Boston Common to begin the operation. An hour later, the troops quietly boarded boats that carried them and their equipment across the Charles River to Cambridge. Gage ordered Colonel Smith to have his men seize the arms and ammunition stored in Concord. The men were told to stuff their pockets with musket balls and scatter them in ponds on their way back to Boston. The British soldiers were also told to destroy any cannons they found in Concord.

The mission the British soldiers found themselves on was so secret that they didn't even know what they were supposed to do. But as the men marched from Boston on the road leading to Lexington and Concord, they heard town bells sounding and shots ringing out. There was no mistaking that something was about to happen.

CHAPTER 3

VICTORY IN LEXINGTON

Early in the morning on April 18, Gage sent 20 of his men on a special assignment. Commanded by Major Edward Mitchell, the men were tasked with stopping any patriots from sounding alarms. But the presence of Mitchell's men was more troublesome than it was helpful.

The men spread out at important points along the roads between Boston and Concord. They talked with travelers they met and asked many questions. One of the questions was where John Hancock and Samuel Adams could be found. But such questions only raised suspicion with the people they encountered.

THE MISSION

Gage chose an elite force of about 700 grenadiers and infantry for his mission in Concord. He put Lieutenant Colonel Smith in charge of the forces. Gage gave detailed orders to Smith: "You will March with the Corps of Grenadiers and Light Infantry, put under your Command, with the utmost . . . Secrecy to Concord, where you will seize and destroy all the Artillery, Ammunition, Provisions, Tents, Small Arms, and Military Stores whatever," Gage wrote. "But you will take care that the Soldiers do not plunder the Inhabitants, or hurt private property."

Hours after leaving Boston, the British soldiers still didn't know their mission. Some thought that perhaps it was just another training exercise. But that thought soon dissolved. Around 3 a.m. they heard shots fired in the distance. Officers who were in the dark about the mission thought it odd to hear gunfire in the middle of the night.

Grenadiers were soldiers trained to carry and throw grenades at the enemy.

Suddenly they heard the sound of galloping horses approaching. It was a group of British officers who had been scouting the road to Concord. They carried bad news. According to Major Mitchell, the whole countryside knew the British soldiers were coming. They had lost the element of surprise. Mitchell reported that he and his patrol had captured patriot messenger Paul Revere but had let him go after taking his horse. Revere had told them that about 500 militiamen were gathered in Lexington, ready to stop their march. The message quickly made its way through the columns of soldiers, who soon realized that this was no training exercise.

Lieutenant John Barker wrote in his diary, "About 5 miles [8 km] on this side of a Town called Lexington . . . we heard there were some hundreds of People collected together intending to oppose us and stop our going on."

ARMED RESISTANCE

Around 4 a.m. dawn began to break and the dark countryside started becoming visible. As the soldiers looked around, they realized they were not alone. Armed men were moving through the fields faster than the marchers themselves.

Eventually the town of Lexington came into view. As the troops moved closer, they saw American Captain John Parker and his militiamen on the village green. As Lieutenant Barker wrote in his diary, "At 5 o'clock we arrived there [in Lexington] and saw a number of People . . . formed on a Common in the middle of Town; we still continued advancing . . . without intending to attack them."

Once in Lexington, Major John Pitcairn ordered the militiamen to drop their weapons. The rebels ignored his order. However, some of them did listen to Parker when he told them to disband.

No one is sure what happened next. Was it a British soldier or a colonist who fired his weapon first? Was the weapon fired at someone else or just up in the air? According to Pitcairn, no British officer ordered his men to fire. He also insisted that he saw 200 armed militiamen, not the actual number of 77. Pitcairn reported that he saw a flash come from behind a wall. Several of his officers agreed.

British Major John Pitcairn (right) was shocked when the militiamen ignored his order to drop their weapons.

The shots fired at Lexington marked the start of the Revolutionary War.

Believing that the colonists had begun shooting at them, the British troops opened fire. "On our coming near them they fired one or two shots, upon which our Men without any orders rushed in upon them, fired and put 'em to flight; several of them were killed," Lieutenant Barker reported.

Pitcairn raised his sword as a signal to stop shooting, but the panicked British soldiers ignored him. By the end of the battle, which lasted less than 15 minutes, eight rebels were dead and nine were wounded. Only one British soldier was slightly injured.

CHAPTER 4

SHOCKING RESISTANCE IN CONCORD

In Lexington, British soldiers pursued rebels who were escaping through yards and fields near the town. "[The soldiers] were so wild they could hear no orders," Lieutenant Barker wrote in his diary.

By the time the soldiers returned to formation and were ready to march again, about half an hour had passed. The officers were divided on what to do next. Some thought they should cut their mission short and head back to Boston. Obviously, the alarm had spread throughout the countryside and their mission was no longer a secret.

PRESSING ON

But Lieutenant Colonel Smith said he had orders from General Gage, and he was going to follow them, so the British pushed on to Concord. When they arrived, they went right to work. They quickly secured the two bridges leading into town—the South Bridge and the North Bridge. One light infantry company guarded the South Bridge. Seven companies were sent to the North Bridge, but only one actually stayed there. Four continued on about 2 miles (3.2 km) past the bridge to the home of American Colonel James Barrett.

Colonists loyal to the British had informed them that a large arms store could be found there. The final two companies held the high ground along the route to Barrett's home—between the North Bridge and the militia.

In the center of Concord, grenadiers searched buildings for arms and war provisions. As ordered, they threw musket balls into a pond and destroyed a cannon they found. They looked for other weapons

Lieutenant Colonel Francis Smith

and ammunition but didn't find any. However, they did find 60 barrels of flour—enough to feed an army—so they dumped the contents into a pond as well.

Some of the British soldiers found wooden carts that were used for carrying large weapons, such as cannons. The soldiers piled them up and set them on fire. The fire quickly spread to a house, which was not what the troops had intended. In an odd turn of events, the soldiers and remaining townspeople worked together carrying buckets of water and pouring them on the house to save it.

At Barrett's house, the troops found nothing of value, but they were tired, hungry, and in no hurry to leave. They demanded food from Barrett's wife, Rebecca, so she gave them something to eat and drink. But she clearly wasn't thrilled to do it. The soldiers offered her money for her trouble, but she refused it, saying, "We are commanded to feed our enemies." When they dropped some silver in her lap anyway, she said, "This is the price of blood."

THE MILITIA MAKES ITS MOVE

Meanwhile, at the North Bridge, the British soldiers who had been guarding the high ground retreated across the bridge as a growing number of militiamen drew near. Three infantry companies now stood opposite the militiamen at the North Bridge. The soldiers were shocked that these country folks had the courage to challenge them. The militiamen were even marching in formation with order and discipline.

Captain Walter Laurie, the senior British officer at the North Bridge, told his troops to prepare to fight. As they scurried to get into formation, the sound of gunfire cut through the air. To his horror, Laurie realized that the shot had come from one of his own men, even though he hadn't given the order to fire.

Suddenly several British infantry members began firing. Most of the shots went high, although some hit their marks. American Major John Buttrick yelled an order to his rebel troops: "Fire, fellow soldiers, for God's sake fire!"

Nine British soldiers, including four officers, were injured in the first volley of rebel gunfire at the North Bridge. The British soldiers quickly realized they were trapped. The Americans were spread out and had clear shots. The British were clumped together, and only the front rows could shoot. Realizing their dilemma, the British turned around and ran toward the center of town.

Realizing they had nowhere to go, British soldiers retreated across the North Bridge.

THE INFANTRY RETURNS

When the infantry returned to Concord from Barrett's house, they quickly realized what had happened. The North Bridge—their only way back to their company in Concord—was unguarded. In addition, a group of militiamen now commanded the hill west of the river where the other two companies of British infantry had once stood. To the east, other rebels held a position on a hill behind a stone wall. The infantry returning from Barrett's house would be easy targets for the rebels if they tried to cross the bridge.

But they had to get across the bridge, so they ran for it. To their shock, they made it across safely. For some reason, the rebels never fired a shot. Not wanting to provoke the rebels, the infantry held its fire as well.

CHAPTER 5

THE RACE TO RETURN TO BOSTON

North of Concord, rebel troops began moving east toward Boston. Smith realized that if the rebels got ahead of them, they could block the route back to Boston. He ordered three companies of troops to the north of the road to keep the line of retreat open. Meanwhile, he got the rest of his troops ready to march.

Placed in horse-drawn wagons, wounded officers were made as comfortable as possible for the journey. The injured who could walk joined their fellow soldiers and tried desperately to keep up. The most severely injured had to be left behind.

The 20-mile (32-km) march back to Boston began around noon and proved to be a nightmare for the British. All along the route, the patriots shot at the British soldiers from behind stone walls, trees, houses, and barns. "[W]e were fired on from Houses and behind Trees, and before we had gone ½ a mile [0.8 km] we were fired on from all sides, but mostly from the Rear, where People had hid themselves in houses till we had passed and then fired . . .," a British Lieutenant wrote in his diary. "[T]he Rebels . . . kept [a nonstop] fire upon us, as we did too upon them, but not with the same advantage, for they were so concealed there was hardly

Hiding behind rocks and trees along the road, the rebels ambushed the British as they made their way back to Boston.

any seeing them; in this way we marched between 9 and 10 miles [14.5 and 16.1 km], their numbers increasing from all parts, while ours was reducing by deaths, wounds and fatigue." The British returned fire but had to be very careful with their ammunition, which was running dangerously low.

Smith sent out flanking parties when the terrain allowed it. The flankers protected the sides of the British troops as they traveled the long road back to Boston. But the rebel forces seemed to be gaining in strength—and numbers.

Just outside Lexington, Captain Parker's group of rebels waited. As Lieutenant Colonel Smith rode with his troops, Parker ordered his rebels to fire. Smith fell from his horse with a bullet to the leg. Though he was badly injured, he later recovered.

The shocked British soldiers stopped for an instant. Major Pitcairn quickly rode forward and sent the infantry charging after Parker and his militia. Both sides suffered casualties, but the ambush was cleared, and the British moved on.

HELP ARRIVES

Soldiers on both sides grew more exhausted as the day wore on. Skirmishes broke out at wells along the roadside as thirsty soldiers fought each other to get water.

Then, as they were crossing into Lexington at Fiske Hill, the British officers lost control of their troops. Some soldiers sat down by the roadside just waiting to die or be captured. Others took off running down the road. Eventually the officers got in front of their men and presented their bayonets. The officers threatened the soldiers that if they did not get into formation, they would be killed. Finally, the troops obeyed.

Some of the officers thought about surrendering. The patriot militia was gaining strength behind them, and just ahead was Lexington's city center. Surely a massacre would await them there, especially since they were running out of ammunition.

Brigadier General Hugh Percy

Then suddenly a cheer arose from the weary troops at the front of the column. In the distance a full brigade of British infantry waited — along with artillery. The reinforcements were led by Brigadier General Hugh Percy. He and the officers with him watched in shock as the exhausted British soldiers made their way to their saviors. "I had the happiness . . . of saving them from inevitable destruction," Percy later said.

Although Percy and his troops were under constant fire on the return trip to Boston, he and his men were able to fight off the rebels. Some of the heaviest fighting happened in the town of

Menotomy, which is now called Arlington. Much of the gunfire came from within houses, leading the tired and angry British soldiers to go from home to home to round up the rebels. "[T]he Soldiers were so enraged at suffering from an unseen Enemy, that they forced open many of the houses from which the fire proceeded, and put to death all those found in them," Lieutenant Frederick Mackenzie wrote in his diary when he returned from the day's battles.

THE BEGINNING OF THE END

The British suffered heavy losses in the Battles of Lexington and Concord as well as during the long trip back to Boston. In all, 73 British were killed, 174 were injured, and 26 were missing. Worse yet, the fighting was not over. The shots fired in the Battles of Lexington and Concord proved to be the first in the Revolutionary War.

Interestingly, British Prime Minister Frederick North had suggested the Conciliatory Proposition to Parliament with the hope that it would satisfy the

Prime Minister Frederick North

American colonists. The Conciliatory Proposition said that if the Americans paid the salaries of the royal officials in the colonies, they wouldn't have to pay taxes. At the same time, North also introduced the New England Restraining Act, which said that the New England colonies could only trade with Great Britain and they could not fish in the North Atlantic. Whether North's proposals would have satisfied the Americans and stopped them from going to war for their independence will never be known. By the time

The Treaty of Paris ended the Revolutionary War and officially gave the American colonies their independence.

the Continental Congress learned of the Conciliatory Proposition in May, the Battles of Lexington and Concord had already taken place, and the war had already begun. Although Congress was still undecided about seeking independence from Great Britain, the proposition was rejected.

The Continental Congress may have been debating independence from Britain, but many patriots had already made up their minds. As Dr. Joseph Warren said before the Provincial Congress just a week after the Battles of Lexington and Concord, "to the persecution and tyranny of his [King George's] cruel ministry we will not tamely submit—appealing to heaven for the justice of our cause, we determine to die or be free."

On July 4, 1776, the Continental Congress adopted the Declaration of Independence. Although this document formally announced that the American colonies were seeking their independence from Great Britain, the matter was far from settled. The Revolutionary War was a long and bloody conflict that lasted until 1783. On September 3 of that year, Great Britain formally recognized the independence of the newly formed United States of America and signed the Treaty of Paris, ending the war.

INDEX

SELECT BIBLIOGRAPHY

The American Revolution: Writings from the War of Independence. New York: Library of America, 2001.

Borneman, Walter R. *American Spring: Lexington, Concord, and the Road to Revolution.* New York: Little, Brown and Company, 2014.

Boston Tea Party Ships & Museum. https://www.bostonteapartyship.com/?s=boston+tea+party&cat=1999%2C342%2C203

Ellis, Joseph J. *Revolutionary Summer: The Birth of American Independence.* New York: Alfred A. Knopf, 2013.

Ferling, John. *Independence: The Struggle to Set America Free.* New York: Bloomsbury Press, 2011.

Fischer, David Hackett. *Paul Revere's Ride.* New York: Oxford University Press, 1994.

Galvin, John R. *The Minute Men: The First Fight; Myths and Realities of the American Revolution.* Washington, D.C.: Potomac Books, Inc., 2006.

Hogeland, William. *Declaration: The Nine Tumultuous Weeks When America Became Independent, May 1–July 4, 1776.* New York, Simon & Schuster, 2010.

McCullough, David. *1776.* New York: Simon & Schuster, 2005.

Slaughter, Thomas P. *Independence: The Tangled Roots of the American Revolution.* New York: Hill and Wang, 2014.

Taylor, Alan. *American Revolutions: A Continental History, 1750–1804.* New York: W.W. Norton & Company, 2016.

FURTHER READING

Hamilton, John. *Battle of Lexington and Concord.* Minneapolis, Minn.: ABDO Publishing Company, 2014.

Mara, Wil. *The Battles of Lexington and Concord: Start of the American Revolution.* Lake Elmo, Minn.: Focus Readers, 2017.

Samuels, Charlie. *The Battles of Lexington and Concord.* New York : Gareth Stevens Publishing, 2014.

Thompson, Ben. *The American Revolution.* New York : Little, Brown and Company, 2017.

CRITICAL THINKING QUESTIONS

1. If the patriots didn't have the alarm system in place, how might that have changed the outcome of the Battles of Lexington and Concord? Use details from the text to support your answer.

2. How did the two sides see the causes of the battles differently?

3. Do you think the outcome of the battles would have been different if the British soldiers had known what their mission was from the start? Why or why not?

December 16, 1773

Angry about a tea tax imposed by Parliament, members of the Sons of Liberty dump 342 chests of tea into Boston Harbor; the event becomes known as the Boston Tea Party

1774

Parliament passes the Coercive Acts, known as the Intolerable Acts in the American colonies; among other things, these acts close the port of Boston and require colonists to allow British soldiers to stay in their homes

April 18, 1775

9:00 p.m.: Dr. Joseph Warren asks William Dawes to alert Samuel Adams and John Hancock in Lexington and colonists in Concord that the British are coming

10:00 p.m.: Warren gives the same message to Paul Revere; around the same time, British troops gather in Boston Common to prepare for a secret mission

11:00 p.m.: British troops begin boarding boats to cross the Charles River from Boston to Cambridge; around the same time, Paul Revere leaves Charlestown on horseback on his way to Lexington and Concord

12:00 p.m.: The British begin their march back to Boston; the fighting continues along the way; by the end of the day, 49 patriots are dead, 39 are wounded, and 5 are missing; the British losses are greater—73 dead, 174 wounded, and 26 missing

July 4, 1776

The Second Continental Congress adopts the Declaration of Independence, announcing that America is now an independent nation, free from foreign rule

September 3, 1783

The Treaty of Paris is signed, officially ending the Revolutionary War

The Split History of the

BATTLES OF
LEXINGTON AND
CONCORD:

PATRIOT'S
PERSPECTIVE

BY BRENDA HAUGEN

CONTENT CONSULTANT:
Walter R. Borneman
Historian and Author of
American Spring: Lexington, Concord, and the Road to Revolution

COMPASS POINT BOOKS
a capstone imprint

Compass Point Books are published by Capstone,
1710 Roe Crest Drive, North Mankato, Minnesota 56003
www.mycapstone.com

LIBRARY OF CONGRESS CATALOGING-IN-PUBLICATION DATA

Names: Haugen, Brenda, author.
Title: The Split History of the Battles of Lexington and Concord / by Brenda Haugen.
Description: North Mankato, Minnesota: Compass Point Books, Capstone, 2018.
  Series: Perspectives Flip Books: Famous Battles | Tete-beche format. | "CPB Grades 4–8."
Includes index.
Identifiers: LCCN 2017043055 (print) | LCCN 2017043443 (ebook) |
  ISBN 9780756556921 (library binding)
  ISBN 9780756556969 (paperback)
  ISBN 9780756557003 (eBook PDF)
Subjects: LCSH: Lexington, Battle of, Lexington, Mass., 1775—Juvenile literature.
  Concord, Battle of, Concord, Mass., 1775—Juvenile literature.
  United States—History—Revolution, 1775–1783—Juvenile literature.
  United States—History—Revolution, 1775–1783—British forces—Juvenile literature.
Classification: LCC E241.L6 (ebook) | LCC E241.L6 H38 2018 (print) | DDC
  973.3/311—dc23 LC record available at https://lccn.loc.gov/2017043055

EDITOR
JENNIFER HUSTON

MEDIA RESEARCHER
TRACY CUMMINS

DESIGNER
ASHLEE SUKER

PRODUCTION SPECIALIST
KATHY MCCOLLEY

IMAGE CREDITS

Patriot's Perspective:
Alamy: Niday Picture Library, 13, Pictorial Press Ltd, 15; Bridgeman Images: National Army
Museum, London/The Battle of Lexington, 19th April 1775, 1910 (oil on canvas), Wollen,
William Barnes (1857-1936), Cover Top, Photo © Tarker, 6, Private Collection/ Troiani, Don
(b.1949), 18, 25; Getty Images: DEA PICTURE LIBRARY, 7, Ed Vebell, 14, Hulton Archive, 20,
UniversalImagesGroup, 27, VCG Wilson/Corbis, 11, 24; GRANGER: Sarin Images, 5; Library of
Congress Prints and Photographs Division: 8, 29; North Wind Picture Archives: Cover Bottom

British Perspective:
Bridgeman Images: National Army Museum, London, 19, National Army Museum, London/The
Battle of Lexington, 19th April 1775, 1910 (oil on canvas), Wollen, William Barnes (1857-1936), Back
Cover Bottom, Private Collection/© Look and Learn, 8, Private Collection/Martin, David (1737-98),
10, Private Collection/Troiani, Don (b.1949), 5, 14, Private Collection/Wood Ronsaville Harlin, Inc.
USA, 17; Getty Images: Bettmann, 21, PhotoQuest, 6; GRANGER: Sarin Images, 24; Newscom:
Picture History, 16, The Print Collector Heritage Images, 27; North Wind Picture Archives: Back
Cover Top; Wikimedia: 26, 28

Printed in Canada.
010799S18

Table of Contents

SOUNDING THE ALARM

CHAPTER 1

On the evening of April 18, 1775, colonists in Boston watched as British troops boarded boats just before midnight. They were crossing the Charles River to nearby Cambridge. Near the top of Boston's Old North Church, two lanterns appeared. The lanterns signaled Paul Revere, a member of the Sons of Liberty, to spread the word that the British were on the move. Quickly, Revere rode through the countryside and alerted others. As he spread the news, other men he encountered jumped on horses and helped get the message to as many colonists as possible.

Two lanterns in the Old North Church signaled Paul Revere that the British were moving out by sea.

The patriots expected that the British were going to raid colonial stores of weapons and supplies several miles up the road in Concord. They also believed colonial leaders Samuel Adams and John Hancock might be arrested. Revere knew he had to warn Adams and Hancock, who were staying in Lexington, as well as the folks in Concord. But with British patrols guarding the routes out of Boston and the road to Concord, Revere knew he wasn't guaranteed to reach either of his destinations.

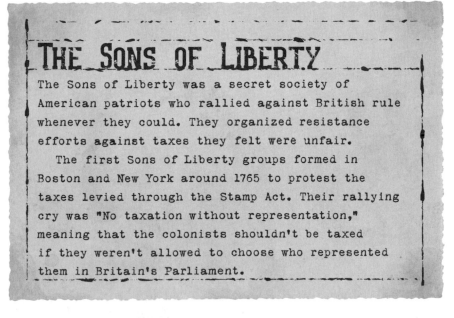

THE SONS OF LIBERTY

The Sons of Liberty was a secret society of American patriots who rallied against British rule whenever they could. They organized resistance efforts against taxes they felt were unfair.

The first Sons of Liberty groups formed in Boston and New York around 1765 to protest the taxes levied through the Stamp Act. Their rallying cry was "No taxation without representation," meaning that the colonists shouldn't be taxed if they weren't allowed to choose who represented them in Britain's Parliament.

GROWING UNREST

In the years leading up to the Revolutionary War, Boston had become the center of growing unrest. Colonists there were fed up with the unfair taxes levied by the British. They boycotted goods that were taxed and had harsh words for the British troops who were sent to enforce the new taxes.

On March 5, 1770, those harsh words turned violent. On that cold New England night, a group of angry colonists insulted a British guard and began throwing snowballs at him. Other British soldiers joined the scuffle and began firing their weapons into the crowd. Five Americans were killed. The event became known as the Boston Massacre.

Tensions boiled over with the Boston Massacre in March 1770. Two of the five victims were only 17 years old.

*In three hours on the night of December 16, 1773,
116 protesters destroyed 92,000 pounds (41,730 kilograms) of tea.*

The Boston Massacre only served to raise the level of anger
many in Boston felt, and it gave them even more reason to protest.
After night fell on December 16, 1773, members of the Sons of
Liberty moved quietly to Boston Harbor. Dressed as Native
Americans, the men boarded three ships docked in the harbor and
dumped 342 chests of tea from the British East India Company into
the water to protest the tea tax levied by Parliament.

Britain's response to the Boston Tea Party was the Coercive
Acts, which singled out Massachusetts—and Boston in particular—
for punishment. Colonists called them the Intolerable Acts. Again,
this move by the British led the patriots to unite. They formed the
First Continental Congress in 1774, which was called to discuss
a plan of resistance that all the colonies could agree upon.

Men, women, and children gathered
to burn the stamps required for certain products.

Armed resistance wasn't out of the question. Since the 1760s

the colonies had been forming Committees of Safety. Made up of

every male in the community, Committees of Safety met to discuss

concerns in the colonies and monitor what the British were doing.

They also controlled local militias, which were ready to fight when

called upon.

CONTROLLING ACTS

The French and Indian War (1754-1763) left Great Britain with a lot of debt. To help pay that debt, Parliament taxed the American colonies. When the colonists objected to the taxes, the British became determined to assert their right to tax the colonies. They responded by passing other acts to exert control.

SUGAR ACT — Passed in 1764, the Sugar Act placed taxes on sugar and molasses imported to the colonies from places such as the French and Dutch West Indies instead of the British West Indies.

STAMP ACT — Passed in 1765, this act taxed all commercial and legal papers, newspapers, playing cards, pamphlets, almanacs, and dice sold in the colonies.

TOWNSHEND ACTS — Passed in 1767, these acts taxed all imported glass, lead, paper, tea, and paint.

COERCIVE ACTS — Passed in 1774 partly as a response to the Boston Tea Party, the Coercive Acts were designed to restore order and punish the rebels in Boston. Known as the Intolerable Acts in the colonies, they included several acts that made colonists angry:

- The Boston Port Act closed Boston's port until the loss of revenue from the Boston Tea Party was paid back.
- The Massachusetts Government Act halted democratic town meetings in the colony.
- The Administration of Justice Act said British officials could not be punished for crimes in Massachusetts.
- The Quartering Act required colonists to share their homes with British troops when asked.

CHAPTER 2

GETTING ORGANIZED

Colonial militias were nothing new in the 1770s. In

Massachusetts, militias had been around since the 1600s. The first

militias formed to protect townspeople from attacks from Native

Americans and foreign invaders. These militias were well trained,

and by the 1770s, many of the men had fought in battles.

The minutemen also traced their history to the early militias.

The minutemen were an elite force chosen from these militias to

respond very quickly. They were expected to be the first militiamen

to arrive on the battlefield.

About one of every three or four militiamen was chosen as a minuteman. They were usually under age 25 and were picked for the job because of their strength and reliability. They needed to be well-armed and ready for battle in mere minutes. The minutemen's ability to be ready in an instant was aided by a series of alarm signals, such as town bells and messengers on horseback. Every community was required to participate in the alarm system.

Paul Revere was part of that alarm system, and he kept a close eye on the movements of the British troops. Not surprisingly, Revere was well known to British officials.

In January 1775 General Thomas Gage, the British-born governor of Massachusetts, received word from his superiors in England. The previous year England's King George III had put Gage in charge of Massachusetts to enforce the Intolerable Acts. Gage was expected to put an end to the rebellion there by arresting patriot leaders and disarming the people of the colony.

Silversmith Paul Revere is best known for his ride to warn colonists, but he also took part in the Boston Tea Party.

SPREADING THE WORD

Because the patriots had important friends in London, they learned of Gage's orders. Not knowing where the British would strike, the patriots prepared to react quickly. They would not make the first move, but they would be ready if the British did. This would give the patriots the moral high ground—meaning that they could say they didn't start the fight. As patriot Samuel Adams said in a 1775 letter, "Put your enemy in the wrong, and keep him so, is . . . wise . . . in politics, as well as in war."

In early April 1775 colonial leaders in Boston noticed that the British Navy had anchored longboats at the back of its ships so they'd be ready for use. Colonial leaders also heard that a group of British officers had been sent to scout out the roads to Concord. The colonists quickly concluded that the British were planning to destroy Concord's store of military supplies.

Word quickly reached Concord, and residents began moving weapons and ammunition out of town to nearby communities. The movements of the British were also reported to Dr. Joseph Warren, another colonial leader. Warren contacted someone who gave him information in times of emergency. According to Warren's source, the British planned "to seize Samuel Adams and John Hancock, who were known to be at Lexington, and burn the stores at Concord."

Around 10 p.m. on the evening of April 18, Warren sent a message for Revere to come over right away. When Revere arrived, Warren begged him to warn Adams and Hancock.

WAS GAGE'S WIFE THE INFORMANT?

Joseph Warren was careful in choosing only the most important times to ask his source for information. The informant was close to the highest levels of the British command, but Warren never shared with anyone who his source was.

Some believe Thomas Gage's wife, Margaret Kemble Gage, was Warren's source. It was no secret

Margaret Kemble Gage

that Margaret felt torn between her loyalties to her British husband and her fellow Americans. Many British officers, including her husband, suspected that Margaret may have betrayed him.

After the Battle of Concord, General Gage sent Margaret to England while he stayed in America. Gage returned to England a year later, but his relationship with Margaret was never the same.

Knowing the British were likely patrolling the roads, Warren had also sent the same message with William Dawes, another member of the Sons of Liberty. Warren hoped that at least one of the men would get through to warn the patriot leaders.

Warren told Revere that Dawes would go on horseback across Boston Neck, a narrow strip of land leading out of the city. Revere planned to take a different route. He would make his way to Charlestown, Massachusetts, where he would borrow a horse from a local patriot.

Revere decided to wait for a signal to confirm the Redcoat's travel plans. Revere had previously arranged the signal with other colonists for this very situation. The signal was simple but effective. When the British made their move, one lantern would be lit in the steeple of the Old North Church if the British were leaving by land. Two lanterns would be lit if the British were leaving by water. Because the Old North Church was the tallest building in Boston at the time, the signal would be clear to those who were looking for it.

Two lights appeared.

Revere went to the north side of Boston, where he kept a boat. Friends helped him cross the Charles River to Charlestown. Once there, Revere borrowed a horse from patriot John Larkin. Revere hopped into the saddle around 11 p.m. and headed northwest toward Lexington.

Paul Revere was part of the alarm system set up to warn colonists that the British were on the move.

Dawes made it out of Boston too. Boston Neck was gated and guarded, but he appeared to be riding a slow horse and looked as if he was just out for an evening ride. The guards let Dawes pass. He likely got through the gate shortly before the guards were ordered to stop everyone from leaving.

Along the route to Lexington, Revere saw two British soldiers on horseback who were guarding the route. When the soldiers saw Revere, they gave chase. Revere turned his horse around and quickly outran his pursuers. But the detour forced Revere to take a different

Revere narrowly avoided capture by British guards on his way to Lexington.

route than he'd planned, and it added more miles to the journey. He finally arrived in Lexington around midnight and delivered the message to Adams and Hancock. Half an hour later, Dawes arrived as well.

The men decided that Adams and Hancock should go into hiding to keep them safe. They also realized that Concord must be warned. As Revere and Dawes left Lexington, the town's alarm bells began to ring, warning the surrounding community that the British were coming.

HEADING TO CONCORD

On their way to warn colonists in Concord, Revere and Dawes met Samuel Prescott, a doctor from Concord who was on his way home from Lexington. Prescott volunteered to help Revere and Dawes warn as many people as possible on the route to Concord.

Working together, the men made great progress in alerting the western side of Lexington. Along the way, Revere spotted a pair of British patrols. He called out to Dawes and Prescott, who were about a third of a mile (0.5 kilometer) behind him. Suddenly, Revere realized there were four British soldiers, not two, and they were well armed.

The patriots tried to rush past the British patrolmen, but they were prepared. They forced the patriots into a pasture, but Prescott got away. He sped off on his horse and disappeared into the darkness to continue to alert the colonists.

As some of the British patrolmen chased after Prescott, Dawes managed to escape as well and made his way to a nearby farm. But when something frightened his horse, Dawes was thrown to the ground, and the scared horse ran off. Without a horse, Dawes walked to the farmhouse only to find it was abandoned. Injured from his fall, Dawes limped back to Lexington, making sure to stay out of sight of any other patrols.

In the meantime, Revere tried to escape into a wooded area. He managed to put some distance between himself and the patrol, but then six more British soldiers emerged from the woods. He was surrounded.

CHAPTER 3

THE BATTLE OF LEXINGTON

By 2 a.m. on April 19 about 130 minutemen had gathered on Lexington's village green. They were led by Captain John Parker, a veteran of the French and Indian War. The men waited but saw no signs of the British. Eventually the men grew cold and tired. Some went home, while others gathered at a nearby tavern.

Just before dawn, a scout spread the news that the British were getting close. Guns were fired and the town bell was rung to signal the militia to reassemble. Seventy-seven men, including Parker, quickly gathered on the town green. Another 40 unarmed residents joined

Minutemen in Lexington were prepared to stand up to the British.

Parker had been told that about 1,500 British troops were headed to Concord, about 7 miles (11.3 km) from Lexington. He ordered his men not to fire their weapons unless the British did so first. "Let the troops pass by, and don't [provoke] them, without they begin first," Parker ordered.

THE BRITISH ARRIVE

Looking down the road that led to Boston, Parker suddenly saw the British troops marching over the hill toward Lexington. They certainly looked like a professional army with their matching red uniforms and shiny weapons. In comparison, the citizen-soldiers of the militia dressed in the clothing of their occupations. They wore farm clothes or the dress of other trades.

The militiamen's weapons were as different as their clothes. The men supplied their own weapons, and they knew how to use them, even though many of the men had no formal military training.

The British quickly reached a fork in the road in front of the Lexington meetinghouse. They were marching fast, but they couldn't miss the militiamen standing on the green behind the building. Instead of veering to the left toward Concord, the leading company of British soldiers went to the right of the meetinghouse. They stopped on the green, right in front of Parker's militia.

British Major John Pitcairn, who was on horseback, ordered the militiamen to disperse. But they couldn't have done so if they wanted to because at the same time Pitcairn gave the order, he also directed his men to surround the militia, preventing them from leaving.

Captain Parker quickly gave the patriots new orders. "I immediately ordered our militia to disperse and not fire," he later recalled.

Some militiamen tried to leave. Others didn't hear Parker's order and stayed in place. None of them put down their weapons.

Suddenly a shot rang out. No one knows for sure who fired first, but John Robbins of the Lexington militia was sure it was the British. "[T]here suddenly appeared a number of the King's Troops, about a thousand . . . at the distance of about sixty or seventy yards from us . . . and on a quick pace toward us," Robbins recalled. "[T]he foremost of which cried, 'Throw down your arms, ye villains, ye rebels;' . . . [one officer yelled,] 'Fire, by God, fire;' at which

Minutemen fired back at British soldiers in what turned out to be the first battle of the Revolutionary War.

moment we received a very heavy and close fire from them; . . . being wounded, I fell, and several of our men were shot dead by one volley. Captain Parker's men, I believe, had not then fired a gun."

Who fired the first shot remains a mystery, but after the British infantry heard the shots, they began firing. Orders from their officers didn't stop them. Spectators who just came out to watch the British troops pass by fled for their lives.

TAKING REFUGE

People in New England did not want to go to war with the British, so when militias from various towns left to aid those in Lexington and Concord, there was no celebration. There was only fear and uncertainty of what was to come.

The country roads around Lexington and Concord were filled with militiamen making their way toward the battlefield. Meanwhile, women, children, and men not involved in the fight fled the scene. Some hid in the woods or in churches. Others went to their neighbors' homes, feeling safer in the company of friends.

The skirmish was over in a matter of minutes, but thick clouds of dirty white smoke from the gunfire hung in the air over the town green. However, it didn't disguise the fact that the patriots had suffered heavy losses. Eight men had died and nine were wounded. One British soldier suffered a minor injury.

Giving a victory salute, the British marched out of Lexington and continued on to Concord. This only fueled the anger of the militiamen who had survived the battle. It wouldn't be the last time they faced the British that day.

CHAPTER 4

THE BATTLE OF CONCORD

hile the battle raged in Lexington, patriots in Concord

prepared for an attack. As word had spread that the British were

coming for the weapons stored in Concord, militiamen from as far as

New Ipswich, New Hampshire—40 miles (64 km) away—arrived

on the scene. By the time the sun rose on April 19, a growing group

of militiamen was armed and ready to face the British on Concord's

village green.

By 7 a.m. news of what had happened in Lexington reached Concord, although there was no report of casualties. About 300 militiamen were sent toward Lexington to meet the British. But when the two groups met, the patriots turned around and headed back to Concord. The British followed, arriving in Concord around 8 a.m. The town seemed to be nearly deserted, but the militiamen were hiding. They had retreated about a mile (1.6 km) away to a hill above the North Bridge. Knowing they were badly outnumbered, the militiamen decided that it was best to wait for reinforcements. Still, from the hill, they were close enough to hear the British grenadiers destroying a cannon, tossing musket balls into a pond, and damaging large stores of flour.

A company of British infantry was guarding the North Bridge — the only path of retreat for the other British infantry groups that had gone farther down the road. One of these groups had passed the militia and gone to patriot Colonel James Barrett's home to search for weapons. Additional infantrymen were stationed on a flat hilltop about 300 yards (274 meters) from the bridge and 1,000 yards (914 m) from the militia. They watched as the number of militiamen continued to grow.

When the militiamen numbered about 500, they decided to move closer to the bridge, advancing toward the flat hilltop where the British infantrymen were waiting. As the militiamen moved closer, the infantrymen left the hilltop and moved toward the bridge.

As the militiamen moved closer to Concord, they saw smoke coming from the center of town. Believing the British had set fire to the town, some militiamen felt it was time for action.

"Will you let them burn the town down?" asked Lieutenant Joseph Hosmer, bravely challenging his superior, Colonel James Barrett.

Barrett ordered the militiamen to the town center with their weapons loaded. He reminded his men not to shoot unless the British shot first. But if they did, the militia was "to fire as fast as [they] could." As the militiamen advanced toward the North Bridge in large numbers, the infantry that had been on the hilltop joined the other Redcoats guarding the North Bridge. They wanted to block the militia's way.

The British opened fire, and two militiamen were struck and killed. The patriots returned fire, killing three British soldiers and wounding nine. Suddenly the British retreated, leaving the bridge unguarded. The patriots watched in surprise as the infantry fled toward the center of town, their wounded "a running and a hobbling about, looking back to see if [the patriots were] after them," militiaman Amos Barrett later recalled.

Realizing that the smoke they saw was just the town's liberty pole burning, the patriots went back across the bridge to treat their wounded and attend to the dead. Gaining confidence as his troop numbers

A group of patriots forced the British to retreat across the North Bridge during the Battle of Concord.

grew, Colonel Barrett decided to divide his forces. He stayed with some men on the hilltop near the North Bridge. Major John Buttrick took another group of men across the North Bridge, closer to the center of town. They gathered on a hill behind a stone wall, a strong position that provided some cover.

When the British infantry returned from Colonel Barrett's house, they ran to cross the now unguarded North Bridge. They were easy targets for Barrett's men on the west side of the river and Buttrick's troops on the east side, but the patriots held their fire. They were still hesitant to start a full-scale war. As it was, the patriots had only fired upon the British because the British had fired first.

By 11:30 a.m. all the British troops were gathered in the center of Concord. The patriots watched the British and waited for them to leave. The British hadn't found as many weapons in Concord as they had hoped they would. Perhaps they were wondering what to do next. Another half hour passed before British Lieutenant Colonel Francis Smith began marching his troops back to Boston.

British troops retreated to Boston after they were defeated by the patriots in Concord.

CHAPTER 5

BATTLING BACK TO BOSTON

The fighting didn't end with the British march back to Boston. All along the route, patriots ambushed the troops every chance they got. Men on both sides were exhausted, but the British forces were at a disadvantage. Their numbers had decreased during the day due to deaths and desertions, while reinforcements from other towns continued to join the patriot militias and minutemen already engaged in the fight. The patriot forces soon included more than 1,000 men.

When the terrain allowed, Lieutenant Colonel Smith sent out flankers—soldiers who were tasked with protecting the sides of the company. When the flankers were called back, the patriots took full advantage. With blood spilled on both sides in Lexington and Concord, the patriots knew that war with the British was now unavoidable. They began shooting as many Redcoats as they could. The British tried to respond, but they had to be careful with their resources because they were running out of ammunition.

Between the towns of Lincoln and Lexington, Captain Parker and his troops waited. Despite their defeat earlier in the day, Parker rallied his troops and they were ready to fight. Some wore bandages covering wounds they'd received earlier in the day.

As the British drew closer, Parker's men waited for the order to fire. Parker had something special in mind. He waited until Smith

As the British marched back to Boston, the patriots hid along the roadside and continued firing at them.

rode up, then he commanded his men to fire. They hit their target. Wounded in the thigh, the British commander fell from his horse.

The surprised British troops stopped for a moment before Major Pitcairn led a charge toward Parker and his militia. Troops on both sides suffered casualties, but the ambush by Parker and his men was deemed a success. From then on, the hillside where Parker's men ambushed Smith and his men has been known as Parker's Revenge.

SAVED BY REINFORCEMENTS

But the revenge was short-lived. In Lexington's town center, British reinforcements under the command of Brigadier General Hugh Percy had arrived along with additional artillery. As the British resumed their journey back to Boston, the militiamen tried to surround them but were unable to do so. The militiamen continued sniping at the British forces all the way back to Boston. For the most part, Percy's men were able to keep them at bay. However, Percy had learned a valuable lesson not to underestimate the patriots. "During the whole affair, the rebels attacked us in a very scattered, irregular manner, but with perseverance [dedication] & resolution . . ." Percy said in a letter to General Edward Harvey. "Whoever looks upon them as an irregular mob, will find himself much mistaken."

When the colonists gathered themselves after the fighting, they discovered that 49 patriots had died, 39 were wounded, and 5 were missing. The British had suffered even more losses—73 dead, 174 wounded, and 26 missing. Although the cost was high, the fighting had proved to the patriots that they could defeat the British.

With the shots fired at Lexington and Concord, the Revolutionary War began. Still, the colonists weren't sure they wanted to be an independent nation.

The Second Continental Congress met in Philadelphia a few weeks after the Battles of Lexington and Concord. Congress raised the question of whether the colonies should declare independence. While fighting continued between the patriots and the British, the debate about independence carried into the spring and summer of 1776, when Congress met again. On July 4, 1776, the decision was made clear when Congress adopted the Declaration of Independence. This document announced that America was an independent nation, free from British rule. Although the Revolutionary War would drag on until 1783, the patriots would finally win their independence, and a new nation—the United States of America—was born.

Members of Congress signed the Declaration of Independence.

INDEX